TOKYO TRAVEL GUIDE

2023

The ultimate and Simplified Guide for

visitors to explore Tokyo

By Alex John

Contents

INTRODUCTION TO TOKYO

Once upon a time, a young woman named Kate wanted to travel to Tokyo, Japan. She'd heard so many stories about the city's culture, fashion, and gastronomy that she decided to take the plunge and explore it for herself.

So she packed her belongings and set off with excitement and anticipation. When she landed in Tokyo, she was struck by its modernism and excitement. There was something new and exciting everywhere she looked, and she couldn't wait to start exploring.

First, she went to the iconic Tokyo Tower, where she enjoyed stunning views of the city. She then spent the rest of the day walking the streets, taking in the sights and sounds of the city. She was taken aback by the brilliant neon signs, the tranquil ambience of the parks, and the delectable aromas of the eateries.

She also enjoyed sampling some of the local cuisine, such as sushi and ramen. She even went out to a karaoke club for drinks, where she had a great time singing her favorite songs.

Kate chose to visit one of the city's many shrines on her final day in Tokyo. The beauty and tranquility of the site astounded her, and it made her feel connected to the city in a way she hadn't previously.

Kate felt a great grief as she prepared to depart, as if she were bidding goodbye to an old friend. She was grateful for the experience she had in Tokyo, which gave her a fresh appreciation for

Japanese culture and people.

Kate had visited Tokyo as a visitor, but she departed feeling as if she had found a home away from home.

Welcome to Tokyo, one of the most interesting cities in the world! Tokyo is a vibrant, buzzing metropolis with a limitless number of things to see and do for visitors. Tokyo has something for everyone, from world-class museums and galleries to landmark temples and shrines, frenetic retail districts to quiet parks and gardens.

Whatever your hobbies are, you'll find something to enjoy in Tokyo. There's something for everyone, whether you're a foodie, a culture vulture, a shopaholic, or a nature lover. The city is home to some of the world's top restaurants, as well as a booming street food culture. At renowned sights such as Meiji Shrine, the Tokyo National Museum, and Senso-ji Temple, you may learn about the city's rich history and culture. There are many lovely parks and gardens to visit, including Ueno Park, Shinjuku Gyoen, and Yoyogi Park.

Tokyo is also a fantastic shopping destination. There are numerous options for people looking for the latest styles, ranging from chic shops to department stores. The city also has a vibrant nightlife, with numerous bars, clubs, and live music venues.

Tokyo has it all, whether you're seeking for adventure, relaxation, or a chance to try something new. So come and learn what makes this beautiful city one of the world's most thrilling places!

CHAPTER 1

HISTORY OF TOKYO

Tokyo, Japan's enormous metropolis dates back to the late 12th century, when the Edo period began. Edo, a little fishing town on the banks of the Sumida River, was the city's beginning. Edo was selected as the seat of the Tokugawa Shogunate, a feudal monarchy that controlled Japan until 1868, in 1457. This marked the beginning of Tokyo's long and varied history as Japan's political center.

During the Edo period, the city expanded rapidly, becoming the world's largest city by 1720. The city was set out in a "grid" style, with large streets and waterways, and was divided into districts by high walls, or "teppos." This era was particularly famous for its emphasis on culture and the arts, which the Shogun greatly supported.

Emperor Meiji moved the capital from Kyoto to Tokyo in 1868, bringing the Edo period to an end. This marked the start of the Meiji period, during which the city grew from a feudal backwater to a significant world power. Tokyo underwent considerable industrialisation and modernization throughout this period. Railways, telegraphs, and other modern comforts were introduced, and by 1900, the population had risen to nearly one million.

During the Taisho period (1912-1926), the city's infrastructure was significantly enhanced with the addition of electric lighting, telephone lines, and other facilities. The city also experienced an increase in foreign influence, with the establishment of embassies, banks, and other companies.

The Great Kanto Earthquake hit Tokyo in 1923, killing over 140,000 people and devastating much of the city. Despite the catastrophe, the city swiftly recovered and began to rebuild.

Allied bombing raids severely destroyed Tokyo during World War II, yet the city survived the fight. Following the war, the city had significant economic growth that continued throughout the 1950s and 1960s. This period saw the establishment of numerous new factories and businesses, as well as the building of a modern public transit system.

Tokyo hosted the Summer Olympics in 1964, enhancing the city's position as a global power. Tokyo has grown to become one of the world's most prominent cities in the decades afterwards. It is now the world's largest metropolitan area, with a population of about 35 million people. It is a major center for commerce, finance, culture, and technology, as well as Japan's political and economic core.

CULTURE OF TOKYO

Tokyo is a city of contrasts, where the ancient and modern coexist together. Tokyo is a metropolis with a distinct cultural identity, from its ancient temples and shrines to its modern skyscrapers and neon lights.

Tokyo's food is one of its outstanding features. The city is famous for its incredible variety of cuisine, which ranges from traditional Japanese meals like sushi and ramen to worldwide favorites like Italian and French. Tokyo has something for everyone, and the city's culinary scene is always developing.

Tokyo is also a fantastic shopping destination. Tokyo is a shopping heaven, with everything from traditional markets and boutiques to the world-famous Ginza and Shibuya districts. Clothing boutiques in the city are especially well-known, with styles ranging from classic to cutting-edge.

The city also has a diverse nightlife scene, with everything from vibrant restaurants and clubs to traditional izakayas and karaoke bars. A robust music culture exists as well, with various venues featuring a variety of jazz, rock, and pop bands.

Tokyo is also home to some of Japan's most recognizable landmarks. From the Imperial Palace to the Tokyo Sky Tree, the city has something for everyone. The city also has some of the country's greatest museums and galleries, including the famed Tokyo National Museum.

In a nutshell, Tokyo is a city of limitless potential, with something for everyone. Its distinct culture is unlike any other in the world and is well worth discovering.

GEOGRAPHY OF TOKYO

Tokyo has the world's largest urban area. It is one of Japan's 47 prefectures, with a population of nearly 13 million people. Tokyo is located in the Kanto section of Honshu's main island, and is bounded to the east by the Pacific Ocean, to the south by the Izu and Ogasawara Islands, and to the north and west by the Kant Plain.

Each of the city's twenty-three special wards has

its own mayor and local government. The capital of Japan is located at the head of Tokyo Bay and is the country's largest metropolis. The Imperial Palace is at the center of the city, which is set out in a grid pattern. Tokyo is a huge metropolis filled with skyscrapers, neon lights, and a plethora of attractions such as museums, parks, and temples.

Tokyo has numerous airports, railroads, and highways, making it a major transportation hub. The city is also a major economic center, with businesses ranging from finance to manufacturing to services.

Tokyo is a lively and cosmopolitan metropolis with a significant national influence. Its attractions range from shrines and temples to modern skyscrapers and neon lights. Tokyo is a fantastic destination with something for everyone.

CLIMATE IN TOKYO

Tokyo's climate is distinct, with hot and humid summers, frigid winters, and distinct wet and dry seasons.

Tokyo's climate is classed as humid subtropical, having four distinct seasons. Summers in Tokyo are hot and humid, with average daytime temperatures reaching 30°C (86°F) and nighttime temperatures dropping to 22°C (72°F). Heavy rains and thunderstorms are prevalent during the summer months, with five to six typhoons moving through the region on average each year.

Temperatures in Tokyo can be cold and snowy in the winter, with average lows of 0°C (32°F). The city receives its lowest temperatures in January, with snowfall falling from December to February. The city has two distinct seasons: wet and dry.

Tsuyu, or wet season, begins in late May and lasts until late July. Heavy rain and humidity can create for exceedingly uncomfortable weather conditions around this time. The city experiences bright and dry weather throughout the aki season, which begins in late August and lasts until early December.

Tokyo has a warm and agreeable climate, with temperatures rarely reaching extreme highs or lows. The city receives the most precipitation during the summer months and the least during the winter. Tokyo is an excellent choice for those seeking a unique climate as well as a bustling and cosmopolitan city.

LANGUAGE OF TOKYO

Tokyo's language is a fascinating combination of

dialects and slang that have evolved over hundreds of years. It is a language that is always changing and reflects the city's history and culture. Tokyo's language is a mash-up of influences from all throughout Japan, as well as from other nations, most notably China and Korea.

The predominant language of Tokyo is Japanese; however the Tokyo dialect has its own distinct traits. It is distinguished by a high level of politeness and formality that is not always found in other parts of Japan. To demonstrate respect for others, Tokyo's dialect frequently employs honorifics and polite phrases. For those who are unfamiliar with the language, this can be extremely perplexing, yet it is a significant aspect of the culture.

Tokyo also has its own lingo, which is popular

among the younger generations. This is especially visible in the way they address one other, employing informal and endearing nicknames. Many of these words have spread throughout Japan and can now be heard in other cities.

Tokyo is home to numerous different languages in addition to Japanese. These include Chinese, Korean, and English, which are widely spoken throughout the city. English is especially popular since it is the language of worldwide commerce and communication.

Tokyo's language is a remarkable blend of dialects, slang, and other influences, making it one of the world's most unique and interesting languages. It is a language that is continually changing and will undoubtedly continue to evolve in the future.

CHAPTER 2

PLANNING YOUR TRIP TO TOKYO

WHEN TO VISIT TOKYO

Tokyo is one of the top cities in the world to visit. However, if you're considering a trip to Tokyo, you should think about what the greatest time to visit Tokyo is.

The optimal time to visit Tokyo is determined by your objectives and interests. Typically, the peak tourist season lasts from late March until early May. If you want to see the city's famous cherry blossoms and participate in the many festivities that take place during this season, this is the finest time to visit Tokyo. During this time, the weather is often pleasant and agreeable, allowing you to explore the city without fear of severe heat or cold.

If you want to visit Tokyo on a tighter budget, the fall months of September and October are ideal. The weather is pleasant, but crowds are thinner and prices are lower. You'll also be able to enjoy the beautiful fall colors and participate in some of the city's autumn festivals.

The winter months of December to February are also ideal for a trip to Tokyo. While the weather can be frigid at times, it is still pleasant in comparison to other places of the world. Furthermore, the city is decked out in festive lights and decorations, making it an ideal time to explore the city.

Whatever time of year you visit Tokyo, you will have the opportunity to enjoy the city's distinct culture and attractions. Tokyo is a city that will constantly leave you wanting more, with its wonderful food, exciting nightlife, and friendly people.

WHERE TO STAY IN TOKYO

If you're going to Tokyo, you'll need to figure out where you're going to stay. Tokyo is one of the world's largest cities, with hotel alternatives to suit every budget. The city has something for everyone, from high-end luxury hotels to budget-friendly hostels.

Tokyo's five-star hotels provide unsurpassed comfort and services for those seeking the ultimate in luxury. For those searching for a premium stay, the Mandarin Oriental Tokyo, the Peninsula Tokyo, and the Ritz-Carlton Tokyo are all fantastic choices. These hotels offer exquisite accommodations, spas, restaurants, and other services.

There are lots of mid-range hotels to pick from if you're seeking for a more reasonable choice. The Grand Hyatt Tokyo, the Tokyo Hilton, and the Hotel New Otani are among them. These hotels provide pleasant rooms, exceptional service, and a wide range of amenities.

There are many hostels and guesthouses in Tokyo for budget tourists. These are typically significantly less expensive than hotels; however they typically feature shared restrooms and minimal amenities. Khaosan Tokyo, Tokyo Central Youth Hostel, and Hostel Canggu are among the more popular hostels and guesthouses.

You can also stay in one of Tokyo's numerous traditional ryokan for a very unique experience.

These traditional Japanese inns provide a one-of-a-kind opportunity to experience Japanese culture and hospitality. Ryokan typically provide tatami-mat rooms, communal baths, and traditional meals.

Finally, for a more modern experience, consider staying in one of Tokyo's capsule hotels. These hotels offer tiny rooms with just enough space to sleep and, in most cases, shared toilets.

Tokyo has something for everyone, regardless of price or needs. You'll be able to locate the ideal location to stay in Tokyo, whether you're seeking for luxury, comfort, or budget.

GETTING AROUND TOKYO

Getting about Tokyo via public transit can be difficult, especially for first-time tourists. Tokyo is the world's largest metropolitan area, with a population of over 13 million people, and its transportation system is equally vast. Tokyo provides a variety of transportation alternatives for seeing the city and its various attractions, ranging from traditional rail networks to modern bus and taxi services.

Walking is a wonderful way to travel around Tokyo for people who like to explore the city on their own. The great majority of Tokyo's streets are well-kept and simple to navigate. Walking is also a terrific way to take in the sights and sounds of the city.

The Tokyo Metro and Tokyo Monorail are two of the city's most popular options for longer distances. The Tokyo Metro comprises nine lines and covers the city in a 250-kilometer loop, whilst the Tokyo Monorail connects Haneda Airport to central Tokyo. Both are convenient and effective. Fares are calculated based on the distance traveled and can be paid in cash or with a prepaid card.

Tokyo also boasts a well-developed bus system, with buses running throughout the city and to several of its outskirts. The fare is determined by the distance traveled, and you can pay with cash or a prepaid card. Some buses also offer student and elderly discounts.

Taxis are another alternative if you want a more private method to go around Tokyo. Taxis are available and can be hailed on the street or reserved ahead of time. Fares are calculated depending on distance and time, and can be paid with cash or a prepaid card.

Tokyo also offers an Eco Bike bike rental scheme. Bikes can be leased from any of the city's Eco Bike stations, with fees according on how much time you use the bike. It's a quick and inexpensive way to move around the city and see its numerous attractions.

For travelers wishing to explore the city, Tokyo offers a number of transportation alternatives. Getting around Tokyo is simple and convenient, whether you like to stroll, use the subway, bus, taxi, or bike.

NAVIGATING TOKYO'S PUBLIC TRANSPORTATION SYSTEM

Tokyo is one of the most interesting cities in the world, and public transit is an important element of moving about. Navigating Tokyo's public transportation system, which includes subways, buses, trains, and trams, can be frightening for first-time visitors. However, with some forethought and knowledge of the system, getting around the city effectively and swiftly is simple.

First, tourists should become acquainted with the key train lines that connect Tokyo's major areas. The Yamanote Line, Chuo Line, and Tozai Line are the principal lines. These lines connect Tokyo's major districts, including Shinjuku, Shibuya, and

Tokyo Station.

Visitors should also be aware of the Tokyo Metro lines, which mostly run underground, and the Toei Subway lines, which mostly run above ground. While the Tokyo Metro lines are more expensive, they provide more frequent service and are more accessible due to the huge number of station entrances.

In addition to the train lines mentioned above, Tokyo has an extensive bus network. Buses are an excellent alternative for guests who need to travel to certain regions of the city. Bus fares are often less expensive than rail fares, but service is less frequent. Visitors should be warned that some buses will not accept cash and will instead require a prepaid IC card.

The water bus is another way to move about

Tokyo. While not as frequent as other modes of public transit, the water bus is an excellent opportunity to see Tokyo from the water and reach some of the city's more distant places.

Finally, tourists should be aware of the available special tickets and passes to assist them go around more effectively. The Tokyo Tourist Pass, for example, provides unlimited travel on most trains and buses in the city for a set number of days. Another popular alternative is the Tokyo Metro 24-Hour Ticket, which provides unlimited trips on all Tokyo Metro lines for one day.

Navigating Tokyo's public transportation system can be intimidating at first, but with little organization and knowledge of the system, getting around the city and exploring all that it has to offer is simple.

TRAVEL REQUIREMENTS TO TOKYO

There are a few crucial needs for individuals contemplating a trip to Tokyo that should be considered before you begin organizing your vacation.

First and foremost, you must ensure that you have a valid passport. All travellers to Japan must have a valid passport that expires at least six months after their intended departure date. Before flying to Japan, you should also check to see if you require a visa. Certain nations are exempt from visa requirements, but others may need to apply for one ahead of time.

Second, before departing for Tokyo, ensure sure you have comprehensive travel insurance. Travel insurance protects you in the event of an accident or medical emergency, as well as for lost or delayed luggage or travel delays.

Third, you should arrange your budget ahead of time. Because Japan is an expensive country, you should ensure that you have enough money to pay all of your travel expenses. Make careful to examine the prices of lodging, transportation, food, sightseeing, and activities so that you can arrange your budget accordingly.

Finally, you should be knowledgeable of Japanese laws and customs. It is critical to be aware of and respect the country's cultural and social norms at all times. One example is the prohibition on smoking and consuming alcohol in public in Japan.

By adhering to these guidelines, you may ensure that your vacation to Tokyo is both safe and enjoyable. Have a fantastic day touring this one-of-a-kind and intriguing city!

CHAPTER 3

EXPLORING TOKYO

MUST-SEE SIGHTS IN TOKYO

With a mix of traditional and modern attractions, it's the perfect place for visitors from all walks of life to explore and have an unforgettable experience. Here are some of the must-see sights in Tokyo that should not be missed!

1. Sensoji Temple: This Buddhist temple is one of Tokyo's most popular attractions and a must-see for any visitor. The temple is surrounded by a bustling shopping area, so visitors can explore the shops and sample traditional Japanese food.

2. Meiji Jingu Shrine: This shrine was built to honor Emperor Meiji, who was instrumental in modernizing Japan and ushering in a new era of prosperity. The shrine is located in the lush Yoyogi Park, and visitors can explore both the park and the shrine.

3. Tsukiji Fish Market: This lively fish market is a great place to try delicious seafood dishes and pick up some souvenirs. The market is also a great place to watch professional fishmongers at work and learn about traditional Japanese fishing techniques.

4. Tokyo Skytree: This iconic tower stands at 634 meters tall and is the tallest structure in Japan. Visitors can take the elevator to the observation deck for a breathtaking view of Tokyo.

5. Akihabara: This is the shopping and entertainment district of Tokyo and is often referred to as "Electric Town". Visitors can find all kinds of electronics, anime, manga, and more.

6. Imperial Palace: This is the home of the Imperial Family and can only be visited on certain days. Visitors can take a guided tour and explore the grounds, as well as view the East Gardens of the Imperial Palace.

7. Shinjuku: This is one of the most popular entertainment spots in Tokyo and is home to a variety of restaurants, bars, and clubs. This is also a great area to explore Tokyo's nightlife.

8. Ueno Park: This is a large park located in Tokyo and is home to a variety of attractions, including a zoo, museums, a shrine, and a beautiful lake.

Whether you're looking to explore traditional

Japanese culture or experience the modern side of Tokyo, there's something for everyone. So be sure to check out these attractions and make the most of your time in Tokyo!

BEST RESTAURANTS IN TOKYO

Tokyo is a foodie's paradise, with a vast range of gastronomic experiences to suit all interests and budgets. The city provides something for everyone, from traditional Japanese food to cosmopolitan specialties. **Here is a list of some of the greatest restaurants in Tokyo for visitors to try.**

The Michelin-starred Ryugin is one of the best locations to go for traditional Japanese cuisine. Ryugin, located in Roppongi, delivers an outstanding range of kaiseki-style dishes crafted with the freshest seasonal ingredients. The restaurant is well-known for its modern spin on classic Japanese foods, and it is the ideal venue for foodies to sample the best of Japanese cuisine.

Sushi Saito is the place to go for sushi. Sushi Saito, located in the upscale Ark Hills complex, is one of Tokyo's most recognized sushi restaurants. Diners may savor perfectly made sushi prepared by some of the city's top chefs here. The restaurant has also received three Michelin stars for the high quality of its food and service.

The Michelin-starred Ristorante Enoteca Pinchiorri is a must-see for Italian foodies. This restaurant, located in the prestigious Aoyama area, serves an outstanding assortment of Italian cuisine cooked with the freshest seasonal ingredients. The restaurant is famed for its modern spin on traditional Italian dishes, and its refined environment makes it the ideal setting for an amazing gastronomic experience.

Nihonbashi, a Michelin-starred restaurant, is one of the best locations to go for an international dining experience. Nihonbashi, located in the heart of Tokyo's business sector, features an outstanding menu of French, Italian, and Japanese dishes. The restaurant is well-known for its inventive use of fresh ingredients, and the setting is ideal for a special event.

Finally, guests should not pass up the opportunity to dine at **Sukiyabashi Jiro**, one of Tokyo's most prominent restaurants. Sukiyabashi Jiro, located in the basement of a Ginza subway station, is famous for its outstanding sushi choices. The restaurant is well-known for its expertly constructed sushi and devotion to traditional sushi cooking methods.

No matter what kind of food visitors seek, Tokyo provides something for everyone. From traditional Japanese delicacies to foreign cuisine, the city's restaurants provide a memorable gastronomic experience. Visitors to Tokyo should visit some of these incredible restaurants to sample the finest of the city's culinary culture.

SHOPPING IN TOKYO

Shopping in Tokyo is an unforgettable experience. Tokyo has something for everyone, from traditional marketplaces to cutting-edge boutiques. Tokyo has it all, whether you're seeking for the latest fashion trends, technology, or traditional Japanese mementos.

Ginza is one of Tokyo's most popular shopping districts. Ginza is home to a plethora of upscale department stores, trendy boutiques, and expensive eateries. It's also a great place to find the latest fashion trends. Visit Mitsukoshi, Japan's oldest department store, and Matsuya Ginza, the main shop of the Matsuya Department Store brand.

Akihabara is the place to go if you want to buy the latest electronics and gadgets. This region is known as Tokyo's "Electric Town," and it is home to hundreds of shops selling cutting-edge technology. Everything from household things to video games may be found here.

If you're looking for souvenirs or traditional Japanese things, Asakusa is the place to go. This neighborhood is well-known for its traditional markets, where you can get a wide range of things at low costs. Asakusa is also home to the well-known Senso-ji Temple, which is one of Tokyo's most popular tourist attractions.

Whatever style of shopping you're looking for, Tokyo has something for everyone. Tokyo has something for everyone, from traditional marketplaces to cutting-edge boutiques. Take some time to explore the different retail districts that Tokyo has to offer. You will not be let down.

CHAPTER 4

DINING IN TOKYO

TRADITIONAL JAPANESE CUISINE

Traditional Japanese cuisine is a type of dining in Tokyo that allows guests to learn about the culture and cuisines of Japan. The cuisine is centered on a wide range of ingredients and techniques, including traditional dishes like sushi, tempura, and teriyaki.

To begin, sushi is a popular meal in Tokyo. Sushi is produced with vinegared rice that is then blended with other items such as fresh fish, veggies, and shellfish. Nigiri sushi is the most frequent sort of sushi, and it comprises of individual pieces of sushi that are molded and placed on top of rice.

Another popular food in Tokyo is tempura. Tempura is a deep-fried meal that is frequently created with seafood, veggies, and other ingredients. The ingredients are lightly battered before being deep-fried till golden brown. Tempura is frequently accompanied with a dipping sauce, such as soy sauce or ponzu sauce.

Teriyaki is a popular dish in Tokyo as well. Teriyaki is produced with soy sauce, sugar, and mirin, all of which are combined and used to marinate meat and vegetables. The items are then grilled or pan-fried until done and the sauce has caramelized.

Aside from these delicacies, there are many additional traditional Japanese dishes available in Tokyo. Udon noodles, soba noodles, miso soup, and yakitori are among them. These dishes are frequently accompanied by a selection of side dishes such as pickled vegetables, grilled seafood, and grilled veggies.

In addition to these cuisines, there is a wide variety of beverages available in Tokyo. Sake, shochu, green tea, and a range of other alcoholic beverages are among them.

Traditional Japanese cuisine allows tourists to learn about Japan's culture and cuisines. The cuisine is built on a range of ingredients and styles, and it provides a one-of-a-kind eating experience for visitors to Tokyo.

INTERNATIONAL CUISINE

Tokyo has something for everyone, from traditional Japanese food to international fare. It can be tough to pick what style of cuisine to try as a visitor. Exploring international cuisine in Tokyo is one of the better possibilities.

Tokyo's international cuisine is broad and intriguing. There is something for everyone, from Italian pizzerias to Mexican taco shops. There are restaurants that specialize on regional dishes from around the world for people looking for an authentic experience. For the more daring, there are fusion restaurants that combine traditional flavors from several countries. Tokyo has a wide range of international restaurants to select from, whether you want a quick lunch or a fine dining experience.

Tokyo's cultural diversity is reflected in its cosmopolitan cuisine. There are restaurants serving cuisine from all around the world. There is something for everyone, from Chinese dim sum to Spanish tapas. Many restaurants provide inventive interpretations on international cuisine in addition to traditional cuisines. Japanese-style Italian pizza, for example, or Korean-style Mexican tacos.

Tokyo is well-known for the high quality of its components. To generate unique flavors, many international restaurants in Tokyo use fresh, seasonal ingredients. The price frequently reflects the quality of the ingredients, but there are lots of low-cost options. Whether you want a quick, cheap bite or a lavish feast, Tokyo has something for everyone.

There are numerous opportunities to sample international food in Tokyo. There is something for everyone, from classic cuisines to inventive fusion food. Tokyo is an ideal location for exploring international cuisine, thanks to its high-quality ingredients and numerous options.

STREET FOOD

One of the finest ways to experience the city's distinct cuisine is through street food. Street food is an important aspect of Japanese culture, and it's an excellent way to sample some of Tokyo's many gastronomic delicacies.

In Tokyo, street food comes in various shapes and sizes. There's plenty for everyone, from modest konbini (convenience store) nibbles to enormous yakitori (grilled chicken) booths.

Regional delicacies like okonomiyaki (Japanese pancake) and takoyaki (octopus dumplings) are available, as are worldwide favorites like ramen and gyoza (dumplings).

One of the best things about street food in Tokyo is that it is usually very cheap. Many of the dishes are reasonably priced, making it an excellent choice for budget tourists. Street food is also a terrific way to tour the city without having to stop for a full meal because it is usually provided on the go.

Street food is also a terrific way to experience Tokyo's local culture. Many of the meals offered at street stalls and kiosks have been made the same way for centuries, and eating them is an excellent opportunity to learn about the city's history and culture.

Overall, street food is an excellent way to sample Tokyo's culinary offerings. It's usually reasonably priced and offers a wide range of diverse dishes to sample. It's also an excellent opportunity to learn about the local culture and history. Street food is a terrific alternative for those who want to explore Tokyo, whether they want a quick snack or a full meal.

CHAPTER 5

ENTERTAINMENT

NIGHTLIFE

When it comes to entertainment, Tokyo nightlife provides something for everyone and is one of the most active and interesting cities in the world. From the neon-lit streets and lively nightlife to daytime shopping, sightseeing, and savoring great Japanese cuisine, Tokyo is guaranteed to keep visitors occupied.

There are numerous alternatives for tourists to Tokyo who want to experience the city's nightlife. There are many of distinctive bars and restaurants offering a variety of music, art, and performance for visitors wishing to explore the city's unique culture. Tokyo's vibrant pubs are fantastic locations to meet residents and get a real sense of the city, while nightclubs offer a variety of music and entertainment, ranging from traditional Japanese music to modern-day dance music.

If you want a more traditional experience, Izakayas in Tokyo are a terrific choice. These traditional Japanese pubs feature a variety of delectable cuisine and drinks and are ideal for socializing and meeting locals.

For those seeking a more casual atmosphere, Tokyo's numerous karaoke bars provide an excellent opportunity to sing and unwind with friends.

For visitors looking to experience Tokyo's vitality and nightlife, the city's many clubs and venues provide a variety of music and entertainment. Tokyo's nightlife has something for everyone, from world-famous DJs to smaller underground clubs. The city's numerous concerts and music festivals are other excellent ways to immerse you in the city's rich culture.

There are numerous possibilities for individuals wishing to experience Tokyo's nightlife in a unique way. Tokyo offers a diverse spectrum of traditional entertainment, from traditional theatre performances to kabuki and noh.

For those seeking something more contemporary, the city's various live music venues provide a variety of performances ranging from jazz to rock, hip-hop to techno.

No matter what kind of entertainment you want, Tokyo's nightlife has something for everyone. Tokyo has a variety of bars, restaurants, clubs, and events to keep visitors engaged day and night.

FESTIVALS AND EVENTS

Attending one of the cities various festivals and events is one of the greatest ways to explore everything it has to offer.

Tokyo is well-known for its diverse festivals, which bring together citizens and visitors to celebrate the city's culture and legacy.

The Setsubun Matsuri and the Sanja Matsuri are Tokyo's two most important festivals. The Setsubun Matsuri, held on February 3rd each year, is a significant event in the Japanese Shinto calendar.

People undertake rituals to chase out evil spirits and bring in good luck during the celebration. The Sanja Matsuri is a three-day celebration held in the Asakusa neighborhood of Tokyo. The event, which includes parades, music, and food, is a celebration of the city's traditional culture.

Aside from these huge festivals, Tokyo is recognized for its numerous smaller events. The Sumida River Fireworks Festival is one of the most popular.

This annual event takes place in July and offers a spectacular fireworks show over the Sumida River. The Tokyo Marathon, Kanda Matsuri, and the Tokyo International Anime Fair are among popular events.

Festivals and events are a terrific chance to immerse you in Tokyo culture and create experiences that will last a lifetime. Tokyo has something for everyone, whether you want to soak in the atmosphere at a traditional festival or enjoy some of the city's more sophisticated events. So, if you're searching for a unique and thrilling experience, make sure to check out Tokyo's many festivals and events.

CHAPTER 6

TIPS FOR VISITING TOKYO

TOURIST TRAPS TO AVOID

With so much to explore and enjoy, it can be easy to get caught up in the excitement and overlook potential tourist traps. To help make sure your trip to Tokyo is as enjoyable as possible, here are some tips to avoid tourist traps in Tokyo:

1. Avoid Eating at Touristy Restaurants: While there are many delicious restaurants in Tokyo, many of them are geared towards tourists and may not offer the same quality of food as local restaurants. Look for restaurants that are frequented by locals to ensure you're getting the best quality food.

2. Don't Buy Souvenirs at Tourist Traps: While souvenirs can be a great way to remember your time in Tokyo, avoid purchasing them from touristy shops. These stores often have overpriced merchandise of questionable quality. Instead, look for souvenirs in local markets or stores that are frequented by locals.

3. Avoid Taking Unnecessary Taxis: Taxis can be an expensive way to get around Tokyo and it's easy to get taken for a ride if you're not familiar with the city. If possible, opt for public transportation such as the metro or buses, as they are much more affordable and efficient.

4. Avoid Being Pressured to Buy Art: Tokyo is home to many art galleries, but some of them can be tourist traps. If you are interested in buying art, do your research beforehand and find a reputable gallery that is not just out to make a quick buck.

5. Don't Fall for Overpriced Attractions: Tokyo is home to various attractions, such as theme parks and museums, but some of them can be overpriced. Do your research beforehand and find out how much things cost, so you don't end up overpaying for something.

By following these tips, you can ensure that your trip to Tokyo is enjoyable and free of tourist traps. Enjoy your time in Tokyo and make sure to take advantage of all the city has to offer!

TRAVEL SAFETY AND SECURITY

Traveling to Tokyo can be an amazing experience, but it is important to consider safety and security when planning a trip. Tokyo is a bustling city with a population of over 13 million people, which can make it overwhelming to navigate. To ensure a safe and enjoyable stay, here are some tips to consider when planning a visit to Tokyo.

1. Familiarize yourself with the subway system: Tokyo has an extensive public transportation network that can make it easy to get around the city. However, it can be difficult to navigate if you are unfamiliar with the system. Before your trip, take some time to research the different subway lines and stations so you can plan your route. Also, consider using Google Maps or other online mapping tools to map out your destination before taking the subway.

2. Stay aware of your surroundings: Tokyo is a large city, and it is important to stay aware of your surroundings at all times. Keep your belongings close to you and be aware of people around you. If you feel unsafe, trust your intuition and move to a different area.

3. Avoid walking alone at night: Although Tokyo is generally safe, it is best to avoid walking alone at night, especially in unfamiliar areas. If you do go out at night, consider taking a taxi or asking a friend to accompany you.

4. Be aware of scams: Tokyo can be a popular destination for tourists, and it is important to be aware of potential scams. Be wary of people offering services or products that may seem too good to be true. Additionally, be aware of pickpockets and do not carry large amounts of cash or valuable items with you.

5. Have a plan: It is important to have a plan in

case something goes wrong. Make sure you have a phone number for the local police and your embassy. Additionally, consider carrying a copy of your passport, as well as important contact information, in case of an emergency.

Following these tips can help ensure that your visit to Tokyo is safe and enjoyable. Taking the time to plan ahead and research the city can make all the difference in having a positive experience.

MONEY MATTERS

To ensure that you get the most out of your trip to Tokyo, here are some money-saving tips to keep in mind:

1. **Make sure to familiarize yourself with the currency system before you go.** The Japanese currency is the Yen, and it is best to get some Yen before you leave for your trip. That way, you can avoid the hassle of exchanging your currency and getting charged exorbitant fees.

2. **Look for special discounts.** Tokyo is full of great deals, from discounted train tickets to discounts on entry to certain attractions. There are also various discount cards available, such as the Tokyo Metro Pass and the Tokyo Tourist Pass, which can help you save a lot of money.

3. **Try to book your accommodation in advance.** This will help you save money, as well as ensure that you get a room in a good location. If you plan to stay at a hotel, compare prices on different sites to get the best deal.

4. Take advantage of the free attractions in Tokyo. There are plenty of free things to do in the city, such as visiting the Imperial Palace, exploring the many parks and gardens, and walking around the city to take in the sights.

5. Consider using public transportation. Public transportation in Tokyo is reliable and efficient, and it is much cheaper than taking a taxi. Take advantage of the train and bus systems to get around the city.

6. When dining out, look for restaurants that offer affordable set meals. Many restaurants in Tokyo offer set meals, which are often much cheaper than ordering individual items.

7. Buy souvenirs at the local markets and shops. Souvenirs from the local markets and shops are usually much cheaper than those from the tourist stores.

Following these tips will help you save money while visiting Tokyo, and ensure that you get the most out of your trip. Enjoy your stay in Tokyo!

CHAPTER 7

MAPS

TOKYO TOWER

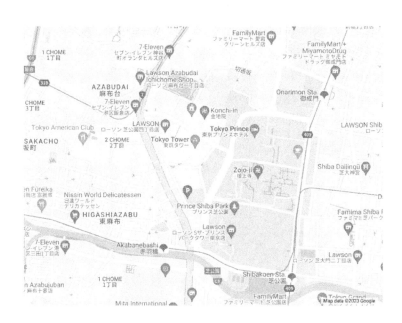

SENSOJI TEMPLE

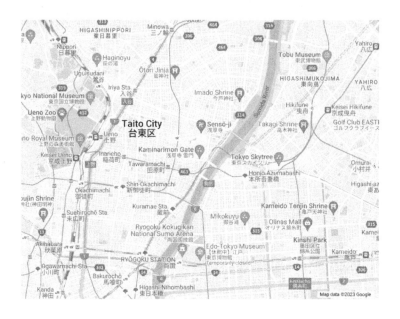

MEIJI JINGU SHRINE

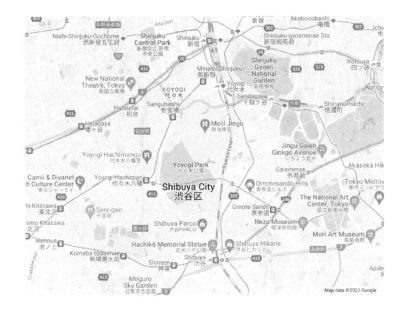

TSUKIJI FISH MARKET

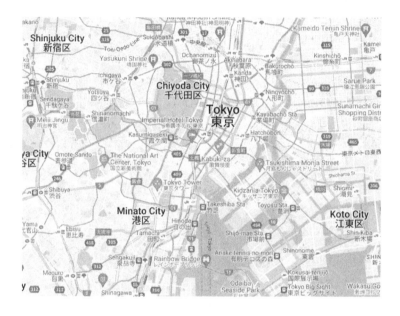

TOKYO SKYTREE

AKIHABARA

IMPERIAL PALACE

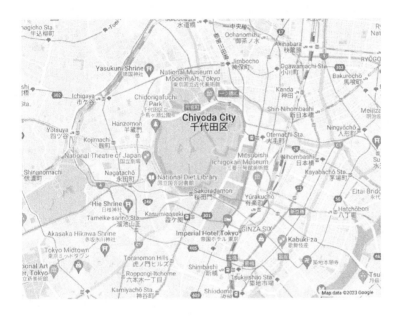

SHINJUKU

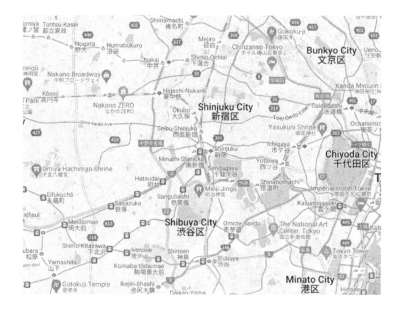

UENO PARK

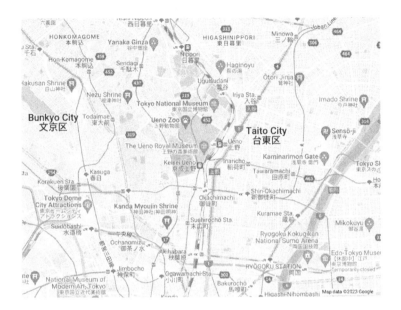

CONCLUSION

The Tokyo Travel Guide 2023 is the ultimate and simplified guide for visitors to explore Tokyo. It has provided an informative and comprehensive overview of the city, from its amazing attractions to its vibrant culture and history.

From the traditional districts of Asakusa and the imperial palaces to the modern and bustling Shibuya and Shinjuku, Tokyo has something for everyone. With its efficient transportation system and friendly locals, Tokyo is a destination that will leave you with unforgettable memories.

Whether you are visiting for business or pleasure, the Tokyo Travel Guide 2023 will help you find the best places to eat, stay, and explore. With its detailed information, you will be able to make the most of your trip to Tokyo. Enjoy your stay in the city and make sure to visit the iconic sights and landmarks while you're there.

Thank you for purchasing my **TOKYO TRAVEL GUIDE 2023!** I appreciate your support in helping me share my knowledge and experience with the world. I hope you enjoy exploring TOKYO. Thank you for believing in me and my work.

Printed in Great Britain
by Amazon

18320414R00047